Unveiling
the
Silent Cries

Sherry Bevill Moss

Mt.Blanco Publishing Co.

Published by Mt.Blanco Publishing Co.
Crosbyton, Texas 79323
mtblanco.com

First published 2015

Manufactured in the United States

ISBN 978-0-9905977-4-2

Forward

This has been the hardest book I have ever worked on and the most difficult illustrations I have ever done. They are not good art, but perhaps they can convey some sense of what Sherry was going through. Robert Mack Moss was my first cousin. His mother and mine were sisters. We grew up together and until I moved back to Texas in 1984, I would have said he was my favorite male cousin and Judy Allen my favorite girl cousin. Judy still is. Robert Mack became very difficult to be around for all of us. But, this was only a tiny fraction of what Sherry and her children were going through. I feel guilty that I didn't know more and do more. God forgive me.

Everything that happened to turn him into the monster Sherry lived with for 19 years, may never be known. However, he was mean even as a child and after high school became a whore monger and a drunkard of his own admission. In 1972 he seemed to have become a Christian and as his brother said, "He went from being the wildest man that ever lived to the most religious man that ever lived." Unfortunately, as this book documents, his conversion was not real. God bless Sherry Moss and her excellent children.

Dedicated to my children:

Con
Caleb
Gideon
Hannah
Elijah
Noah
Micah
Enoch

Contents

My Sustainable Scripture
My Scripture of Hope Today
Are You a Victim
Notes
Acknowledgements

CHAPTER ONE

What Should Have Been A Special Time

Journal entry August 10, 2007

This is the beginning of trying to start putting my life of the last 27 years down on paper. I have thought about doing this for years but this year I have decided to step out and get going. Not sure if I am writing this for myself, my children, family, or praying my words will encourage some one who is going through the same dreadful days I went through. I remember only a few times when I truly have been happy.

From 1998 to the beginning of this writing have been pure heaven. Not saying there have been many ups and downs and wondering if my children and I could survive. The closeness and the children and I have, has kept us strong. And know that the prayers that have gone up for our family have provided us with the knowledge we all can be conquerors in the battles. And our life up until 1998 was truly a war zone each day that we got up. How does one start a book. And especially one like this.

But I am going to back up to 1980 the year I met my husband, which was a fast paced relationship, and should have been taken slower. But even then as I look back he had control of me. And from the time I said "I do", was the beginning of me saying "I am sorry", even if I had done nothing wrong. I never remember doing anything that down deep that ever pleased him. For many times he said "he didn't know one thing I could do right". He said I couldn't even have children right.

2

Years 1980, 81, 82, 83, 84, 85, 88, 1991, 1997

These are the years I wanted my family to intervene. They did not. Either the plans I made fell through or Robert Mack found out. Either way, I stayed trapped in a marriage built on fear and control. Horrific abused followed if I tried to leave.

The times I remember the most were life threatening events. His hand around my throat squeezing so hard I couldn't breathe or a knife held to my throat were frightening experiences repeated often. "I need to just slit your throat and get rid of you. Cut you up, throw you away and let the dogs eat you and drink your blood," he'd shout." He'd beat me in the back until the pain would literally take my breath away. Then overcoming the pain took everything inside me to function so the children wouldn't know what he had done.

He always made sure he hit me at night when they were in bed or outside where they wouldn't hear anything. I would get down on my knees and cry so hard I couldn't breathe. My crying had to happen when no one could hear usually at night when I took a bath. Finally, I could cry. The water muffled my crying. My deepest time of prayers to God flowed with my tears. God was giving me strength daily and carrying me through.

How many times did I say I was sorry? How many times did I say I will do better? How many times did I say everything was my fault? What I said didn't mattered to him. He tried to make me believe my words mattered. If he thought I believed he cared about my words, this let him off the hook and meant sex. He could hardly go one day without sex.

Having everything that happened my fault became an obsession with him, but he maneuvered so that everything appeared all right just long enough to have sex. Then, he'd order me outdoors for the night.

At some point between 1988 and 1991, I told Robert Mack's parents I couldn't take it anymore. With four children and pregnant with my fifth child, I spent night after night trying to figure out a way to leave. My escape had to happen during the day when Robert Mack worked on the farm. Robert Mack's dad gave me $200.00 cash to fill the Suburban with gasoline.

I'd decided to drive to Tom and Kathy Taylor's home less than two hours away where we'd be safe. After the days of agonizing planning, the children and I were ready to leave. Robert Mack came home before we left. I feel that his parents let me down thinking they could improve their own relationship with him. Later, they made a statement about making sure nothing would happen to us, but those were only words. As I look back, their control becomes obvious. One positive opening remained. Robert Mack never knew about Tom and Kathy's willingness to help us. My last and final attempt to leave happened in 1998. This story will follow later in the book.

Journal entry
I am just an ordinary person. A woman who thought I had found the man of my dreams. And each day a little of my dreams, of my life was taken away by a man whom I thought would love and protect me every day. In the years that laid ahead of me, I had 8 wonderful children! And during all this time heaven only knows how I kept it together so that they would be born safely. The children had so many daily obstacles and I mean every day.

Our wedding day Nov. 22, 1980

My married life began on November 22, 1980. What should have been a special time in a girl's life didn't feel very special. He didn't want my Church of Christ background influence involved in the wedding. I chose who married us and who sang at the wedding, but that was all. On our honeymoon I remember telling him I didn't want to make love anymore, because that's all we did. I was a virgin, and the rough sexual activity hurt. I learned a hard lesson that day. My new husband informed me he had a God given right to have sex anytime he so desired. He quoted the scriptures arguing his point. Soon I began to doubt everything I knew about the scriptures. The enormous control had begun.

After returning from the honeymoon trip, we had a big argument one evening. While he was in the shower, I left quietly and drove to my church. I called and met with an elder. Robert Mack followed me. He talked nicely to the elder at the church, but he wasn't so nice after we returned to the apartment. From that point on, he would not let me have a choice about anything, not even my religious beliefs. He made sure I only said what he told me to say. Not complying meant trouble.

I met Robert Mack through my Aunt Laura Faye. I had moved from Lubbock to Greenville to work for my aunt in her cleaning business. She cleaned the fertilizer business Robert Mack managed. Because he worked late one evening, I met him. We talked a few other times at the plant. My aunt and uncle thought well of him at the time.

Our first date was to the Dallas State Fair. I thought attending the fair was cool. Both of us wore blue shirts, jeans, and boots. When we returned to my apartment that night, he was a little forceful. I stood my ground and said no, because I really didn't know him. He began taking me out to eat and buying me some nice things. Once at K-Mart he bought me four dressy hats for church. I told him how much I liked hats and that my daddy always liked me in a hat. I thought this man was sure nice. He said, "If your daddy likes you in hats, then you deserve to have them." We continued eating out, and we were invited for dinner with my aunt and uncle a few evenings. Then, one night we had a huge argument. He made some statements that should have stopped me period. I should have stepped back and wondered if I really wanted this relationship to continue. A few days later he wanted to see me, and he apologized. But, a few days later he brought up the argument again. "I shouldn't have said I was sorry because you were the one in the wrong, not me." Red flag! But, I didn't heed it!

He began speaking to me about how I dressed, my make-up, my jewelry, and my short hair. I wondered what he liked about me. He dropped the topic and said never mind. "I have fallen in love with you, and it doesn't matter." I thought he was accepting me for being me.

The middle of October he left on a hunting trip to Colorado with some of his long time hunting buddies. He called me every night, sent me post cards telling me how much he loved me, and how he couldn't wait to get back to Greenville to see me. After his two week trip, he came directly to my apartment and asked me to marry him. I knew he was different in some ways, but I put those thoughts out of my mind. Looking back, he made many decisions without asking me even before we married. For instance, he informed me our wedding rings would be wide gold bands without diamonds. He thought they were attractive and drew less attention. At least that was the reason he gave me. Eventually that ring was all the jewelry I was allowed to wear. He chose my wedding dress, a wool winter white suit. The top under the jacket couldn't be too revealing. He picked out the songs. My college roommate flew in to sing, for which I was grateful. Since I attended Peach Grove Church of Christ at the time, he allowed Phil Tipton to perform the ceremony. That was the last time he allowed me to attend the church of my upbringing.

Robert Mack controlled just about everything from the very beginning. I know deep inside me I should have stopped and left the relationship. But, with hope in my heart, I told myself everything would be fine once we married. Man! What stupid thinking! At 25 I was pretty clueless about a lot of things. I thought I had fallen in love with him.

When I met his mother and daddy, they tried to tell me that Robert Mack was hard to get along with. For even that weekend Robert Mack and his dad got into several arguments. His mother would stop them and say, "That's not the way for grown men to act."

6

A few times Martha Lou tried to tell me about some of Robert Mack's lady relationships. He had lived with a couple of women but never married. They couldn't live with Robert Mack's harsh ways, and that's why they wouldn't marry him. However, Martha Lou didn't give me any of these details before our marriage. She did share more details with me through the years after she saw some of the ways Robert Mack treated me when we were out with other people.

Before we married, Robert Mack tried to convince his parents and me that he had turned his life over to God, and he wasn't the same man he'd been with those two other women. He definitely had convinced his parents. Now, as I write this I see he was an evil man to these other women as well. How I wish his mother had shared some of these facts about these women before we married. But, again, he had convinced his parents.

A few weeks before we got married, his parents visited Robert Mack's brother Jerry in Dallas. They drove to the fertilizer plant in Greenville to meet me. They reminded me of my parents in some ways, and I thought they were very nice. We ate dinner in Dallas, then returned to Greenville where his parents and brother stayed in a hotel.

They returned in November for the wedding. Even the night before our wedding day, Robert Mack, his brother, and parents had a big argument about Christmas. Robert Mack said Christmas was a satanic holiday and was determined to show he was right. His mother stepped in to stop the argument.

After the wedding we drove to the Lake of the Pines for our honeymoon. The piney woods country around Jefferson and Marshal was beautiful. I tired of not being able to say no to the sex part. A persistent thought ran through my mind. "Will this man ever get enough?" He would just say, "This is the way it's supposed to be. God has given woman to man." At this point the Bible was used to get whatever Robert Mack wanted.

Alone

Robert Mack moved his things into my apartment for it was nicer than his. Life rolled along fairly well until I asked about attending my church. I thought I could attend Pecan Grove Church of Christ, he could attend his Baptist church, and we could meet back at the apartment after church. He said I would never attend Pecan Grove church or any other Church of Christ. He was the spiritual leader in the home, and I would do what he said. We began attending Ridgecrest Baptist Church and continued for almost a year.

I know I've mentioned the sex thing previously, but it mushroomed into a huge dark cloud over our relationship. Robert Mack used the Bible to get all the sex we wanted from me. I could never tell him no. This should have made me more aware of problems about Robert Mack. I should have asked his mother for more information concerning his female relationships.

8

His aggressive actions toward sex and the every day requirement hurt me physically and drained me emotionally. Most days he wanted sex two times a day and some days more often. The oral sex was awful. I wanted to throw up every time he made me have oral sex. He never ever had his fill of sex. He used ugly words, nasty words, and cuss words during sex. On the outside, he would condemn this type of language, condemn oral sex, and state how wrong for Christian people to mention such sex acts in adult conversations.

Because they were hiring someone new to manage the fertilizer plant, the company discharged him. However, that was not the truth. They actually fired him. He lied to me. I didn't find out about the lie until years later; he still denied they fired him. He said they were all liars and were in the wrong. Funny that I was the one he always called the liar. But, more and more through the years I found out about lies upon lies from his lips.

He was called to Houston where the company informed him of his job loss. The management job for Occidental Fertilizer had ended. Robert Mack applied for a salesman's job with Center Plains Fertilizer in West Texas. We moved to Crosbyton, Texas. Robert Mack always wanted, or so he said, to be closer to his cousin Joe Taylor. Someone in his family found out about a house in the country. He wanted to live in the country, and that was fine with me.

CHAPTER TWO

Little Did Anyone Know

We lived in a nice country home fourteen miles from Crosbyton, two miles off pavement. Robert Mack worked as a salesman for Central Plains Fertilizer and traveled all week. These times should have been hard on a new wife, but I learned to take those times alone and really enjoy them. His family lived close by, and they were good to me. They were glad Robert Mack had met someone who could turn him around. Supposedly, several years previously, he experienced an awakening and was a real Christian person now.

He made me sleep outside many nights at our country home even when I was pregnant.

Little did anyone know he was still the same wild and controlling man. I had a chance to ask one of Robert Mack's female cousins about sex. She told me in no uncertain terms that sex should not hurt but bring pleasure to the woman. The sexual aspect of our marriage continued as an ongoing problem.

I did travel some with him as he called on fertilizer dealerships. I looked forward to the Big Bend area, but what should have been good time turned into a disaster. Once he locked me outside the hotel room, and told me I would have to sleep outside. I suppose he thought someone might notice, so he let me back in the room to sleep on the floor.

On another trip to the Big Bend area, I had to sleep in the car at the hotel. He didn't like something about my attitude. I had no idea why. The next morning he went for coffee and told me to go inside and get ready. He also ate breakfast, but I didn't get any. We left and drove back to Crosbyton without a word spoken the entire distance. When we arrived home, he said I should have apologized enabling us to talked on the way home.

journal entry

I had been married for awhile before Robert and I got married, but the marriage was annulled, and I think this always made him angry and he never wanted anyone to know. And he said I was never to talk about it or tell anyone. And if we ever had children, they would never know about it. The marriage was never consummated. The man knew he could never be the husband that could make me happy. Enough of that.

The road to our house was one of the worst stretches of dirt road in Crosby County. People didn't want to travel that road if it rained or snowed. Even the big farm tractors would get stuck. In the winter the mailman reversed his route so he could travel our road in a frozen state. Otherwise, even the mailman got stuck.

Not long after we moved to the country, Robert Mack said he was going to teach me how to drive the Bronco. It was a standard shift. I'd never learned to drive a standard shift. He began teaching me, and I knew this would be a bad situation

journal entry

Robert Mack would get very mad if I didn't learn from the get go. And I was right at first. He tried to not get upset. Then he decided I wasn't really trying. So the first thing he did was pinch a couple of places in my rib area. Took out some skin with each pinch which was 5 or 6 places. Then he started slugging me on the upper part of my arm close to the point of my shoulder. Then a couple of slugs went against my right ear. Then he took my right ear and twisted while telling me I would learn. Finally made it to his cousin's house which was only a few miles from ours. But we stayed later and he drove home. The next day he had to make sales calls to fertilizer companies so he was going to be gone for several days. And while he was gone it rained so I drove the Bronco down to the end of the road and then a little ways up the highway to leave it at the Hodges' House. Also the same people who owned the house we were renting. And then I walked back to our house which was about 2 ½ miles. When he returned home after a few days, he drove the Bronco home.

We attended the Crosbyton First Baptist Church. The family thought all was well within our home. I tried to make sure that's what people thought. We had social gatherings at some of the church couples' homes. These times brought a bit of happiness into my life. After Christmas we went to Cloudcroft, New Mexico, with this Sunday school class.

journal entry

While we were on the trip everything seemed to be great. Robert Mack was very caring and loving. Which was a real welcomed change. We went in the church vans. And on the way home Robert Mack wouldn't say anything to me. Got home and he started telling all the bad things I did wrong while on the trip. Didn't do anything that was all right towards him he said on the whole trip. Tried to get him to pinpoint what I did wrong and then he started in on that he couldn't discuss with me for all I wanted to do was argue. And I slept on the couch that night. And we kind of thought I might be pregnant. So I made an appointment with Robert Mack's cousin's doctor in Lubbock, Dr. David Rogers.

12

On the 25th of December 1982, we conceived our first son. I thought finally something would please him and make him feel better about me. We had been trying to conceive. Robert Mack kept telling me it was my fault we couldn't. I began thinking it was my fault. Maybe I couldn't do anything right like he said. Maybe I wasn't being submissive enough to him. When we were to visit the doctor to confirm the pregnancy, there was a fight. Finally, he let me go in the house and clean up. At two months pregnant, I slept outside for the first time.

He poured hot coffee down the front of my shirt

Although I thought he seemed in a nicer mood the next morning, I didn't say something right. ***He took the hot pot of coffee on the coffee maker and poured the coffee down the front of my shirt.*** I pulled the shirt off so quickly, it made no blisters. But, the doctor asked me what happened because of the redness. I had to lie about how I got the coffee on me. For a couple of days after that episode, Robert Mack was pretty nice. Actually, for a few months life was pretty calm. We still had ups and downs, but nothing drastic. Robert Mack seemed so excited we were going to have a baby. He took me to eat after my appointment, then to shop for maternity clothes and some items for the baby's room. When we returned home from Lubbock, we called my parents and Robert Mack's parents. Martha Lou was excited because we found out on the day of her birthday. Things went along pretty good for awhile.

13

About four months into my pregnancy, I had cooked black-eyed peas for supper. He came in the kitchen and asked me about balancing the checkbook. That morning he had asked me to balance it, but I hadn't found time. He said, "You've had all day."He picked up the pan of peas and dumped them on the floor. "You can sweep and mop after you've licked up and eaten enough to learn your lesson."

I was a few months pregnant when he made me change the tire

Then one day he decided I needed to learn how to change a flat on the T-bird. I was a few months pregnant. I tried to explain that in my condition, I needed to learn this later. He said I needed to learn how because he said so, and he would make me stay outside until I did as he said. I started trying to change a tire, but he said I wasn't doing it correctly. I just sat down on the porch because I didn't feel very well. He told me to get up. I asked if I could wait until I felt a little better, but he said no. He grabbed me by the arms and stood me up and said, "You get busy, you bitch." I said, "No, until you ask me nicer." He grabbed my shirt at the bottom and jerked. All the buttons popped off.

journal entry

And he went into the house and locked the doors. So I made up my mind to go ahead and change the tire. Got it done.

I knocked on the door of my own house so I could tell him I had finished with the tire change. He came out and saw that I had finished and put everything away. This was almost dark by now. And said I couldn't come back in the house to sleep and he locked all the vehicles so I couldn't sleep in any of them. And the doors to the house he locked also. I found a 5 gallon bucket and just leaned up against the west side of the house. He didn't come out until the next morning and when he left for work and was gone for several days calling on fertilizer plants.

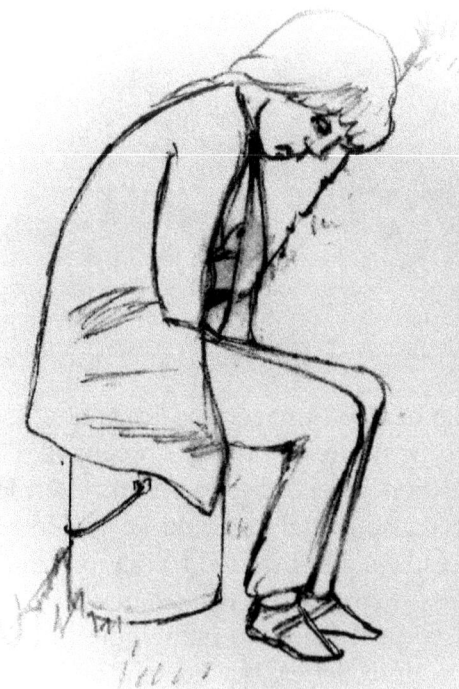

He mad me sleep outside on a bucket all night

Con, our first son, was born. I experienced hard, long labor pains and tore badly during his birth. Recovery was not speedy. My parents came for a few days. How I treasure those memories. They're leaving brought a sad day for me. When they left, the calm was gone. The next Sunday after the evening service, we returned home and something upset him. I was sitting on the couch nursing my son. All of a sudden, he began kicking the front of my shins up and down each one.

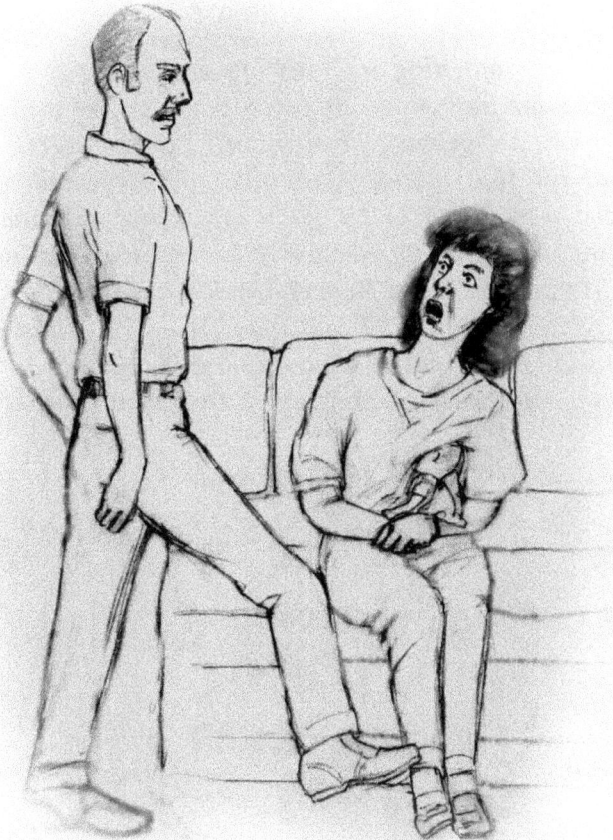

He began kicking the front of my shins

I still wore pants at that time. The pant leg material protected me somewhat, but I still had bruises. He knew where he to hit me to avoid noticeable marks.

I finally put Con in his crib and walked toward the bedroom to hopefully sleep. Robert Mack said I couldn't go to bed until I said I was sorry. As usual, I didn't know what I had done. Because I needed to rest, I said I was sorry. When I laid down on the bed, he slugged me in the back several times and said I'd better straighten up. He called me a slut and a bitch.

journal entry

The next morning he's telling me he's sorry. And he started telling me how much he loved me and Con and how if I would be more submissive he wouldn't get so angry. He did pretty good for the next few months. The company he was working for was going to let go a lot of the salesmen. But Robert Mack wanted to move back to Memphis, Texas and farm anyway. My brothers and Robert Mack's aunt and uncle from Memphis came to help load and move us. We found a house that was on the last street in town that had 3 ½ acres in the back of the house. And we lived there from December 1983-1998.

CHAPTER THREE

The Tyrant

journal entry

When we went back to his hometown to farm and raise our family, life was very hard. The first 8-10 years he worked hard and made a good hand at farming. Then he started finding fault in the people whom he rented farm land from. The government was all in the wrong. The police department had no right to tell him what to do, and no one had the right to tell him how to run the family. And the children and I had no voice at all.

We soon moved to Memphis when Con was only a few months old. After we moved, Robert seemed to be really happy and things were good for nearly a year. But, when Con was a year old, we found out for sure we were having another baby. He was mad blaming me for letting it happen so quickly. I could NEVER tell him no! At that time I was using protective measures, but those preventions didn't always work out. Caleb brought joy to my heart. He came quickly. Even with my parents at our house, I had to push Robert Mack to leave for the hospital. He was determined to take his time. He took me and left to deliver papers his dad needed to sign. Caleb was born before he returned on April 17, 1985. He was mad I didn't wait! His peeved attitude soon disappeared and home life stayed calm for awhile.

During this time we were going to church with his parents, but he complained about how he disliked the preacher. The deacons invited him to consider being a deacon. Some of the deacons talked to us together and then separately. I slipped and mentioned my previous marriage that had ended in annulment. That didn't matter to them. He could have still qualified, but he was upset they knew what he considered a secret. So now everybody would know. His parents thought he just didn't accept the position of deacon. Robert Mack had warned me about keeping quiet. Shortly after that episode, we attended another church in Memphis. I tried to settle into a routine with two babies in diapers. We were going to church, and Robert Mack was working hard. Then, in 1986 our third son Gideon was born. My parents stayed with us a whole month before he was born. My daddy was the one who took me to the doctor. After his birth, they stayed only a few more days.

We planted a big garden

Robert Mack and I planted a big garden. I worked in it when the boys were asleep. Robert Mack did most of the planting, but I did the picking and canning. I was expected to can everything.

journal entry

We had several acres that we raised just about everything we ate. Not saying this is bad, it was just the way it was handled. The older boys could never hoe, water, or pick the garden right. I have stood on my feet sometimes from sunrise until 12 at night trying to get garden vegetables put away. The more I tried to do all I could to take care of the family it was never good enough. There were many times I was canning long hours and I would be 6-9 months pregnant. Or I would have just had a baby and would be stopping during all of this and would stop and nurse one of the babies that may have been born. Never seemed to be any let up time. So grateful for being able to nurse my children for I had some quiet and peace time for 30 minutes at a time off and on during the day. Said a lot of prayers and cried a lot of tears during this special time with each of my children when they were babies.

During the time Gideon was born we were attending a Baptist church in Wellington about 14 miles from Memphis. He thought this church would work for us. I actually made some good friends. After Gideon's birth, they gave us a large baby shower with money and clothes gifts.

journal entry

And when I got close to someone that I could share with he would sense that and he would fix it so that we wouldn't make contact. We never went to church anywhere very long. Because eventually people would figure things were not what they seemed and we would go back to having home church for he could control that. For if he got upset at me at home he could stand me or one of the children in the corner and he couldn't do that at a church.

We attended a Bill Gothard Seminar. After that Robert Mack said no to any kind of birth control. Bill Gothard talked about children being a glory to the Lord and an honor to a man who had his quiver full of children (1). Robert Mack decided we would have "as many children as the Lord blessed us with." It was during this time that Gideon was born. Gideon was born quickly, also. Thankfully, my three baby boys were such good babies. Then, I became pregnant again, but I miscarried. With the ups and downs connected to children and having babies, Robert Mack angered easily making life more difficult for all of us. I became pregnant eleven times, three of which ended in miscarriages. * (1)

When Robert Mack told me he wasn't going to shave anymore, and that I would no longer wear pants, makeup, jewelry or cut my hair, a lengthy fight ensued between us. An adult discussion could never happen. He did most of the talking. I reminded him of what he said when we first married about liking me for myself. Did he believe the restrictions he was imposing on me really came from the **Bible**? Here was the absolute clincher. He said it didn't matter! I should not argue with him period. I did ask him a question. "Do you like anything about me?" To which he replied, "No." He enforced his rules over me and often reminded me, "I can get anyone to do what you do. You'll be out the door with your throat slit if you don't do what I say."

You'll be out the door with your throat slit

During those years, I often stood at the kitchen sink working and assuring him I wasn't arguing or disputing his word. Without warning he would hit me in the back or kick me on the shins with his steel toed boots. What I said didn't matter. He hit me when he wanted to hit me.

A few times he slit my throat enough to make it bleed. He said I must submit to him when I didn't know how to submit any further. He grabbed a kitchen knife from the wooden knife block and held to my throat. I never knew if he intended to draw blood. "I'm going to slit your throat, take you out, and let the dogs lick up the blood."

He's taken both hands and slapped me on the ears as hard as he could until they bruised. Slapping my ears at the same time made them ring fiercely. How I survived without hearing impairments, only God knows.

I have been spit on and called a bitch in the same sentence. He forbade me to wipe away the spit. Only at his command, could I clean my face.

Standing me in the corner for an hour at a time reduced me to a child's level. Again, the reason given included the word **submit.** If treating me like a child was what he had to do in order for me to submit to him, then that's what would happen. Other times I could only leave the corner when I needed to nurse a baby.

He spit on me

Days and days of unrest followed me around like a monster. I wasn't doing enough and wasn't submissive enough as a Christian wife. Gideon hadn't reached his first birthday yet meaning I cared for three small boys. Robert Mack finished plowing for the day and came in the house. As soon as I opened my month, he became unglued. Whatever I said didn't suit him.

He picked up a large potted plant of ivy and threw it hitting the center of my back. Dirt and ivy flew everywhere. After I cleaned the mess, if he saw any dirt, he slapped me on the back or on the face.

He hit me with a large potted plant

journal entry

The last few years we farmed or he tried to farm, he used to go to Amarillo to get things in bulk at Sam's. I stopped going. It was hard on me and the younger children. Every time we went to Amarillo he would say to me that I acted so stupid and acted like someone else. The problem was I would be a little like myself and wasn't the person he had turned me into, which was a slave.

I became pregnant again before Gideon was a year old. Robert Mack became angry more often. For no apparent reason, he would start yelling at me and calling me names. One day he told me I wasn't doing enough to make the home a strong Christian family. He said I wasn't being the right kind of wife. On this particular day I had baked bread, which I did two and three times a week. He thought this loaf crumbled too much. After he sliced a piece, he took a knife to my throat and brought blood. If I recall correctly, this was the first time he told me he needed to cut my throat, take me outside, throw me to the street, let me die, and let the dogs lick my blood. Not long after this I lost the baby I was carrying.

For about 3 months several of the couples from the Wellington church came to see us offering to help. We never attended that church again. We began having home church for the first time. At times we drove to Crosbyton to attend church with Robert Mack's cousins Joe and Tom Taylor.

The fifth pregnancy in 1987 became our daughter, the Lord's gift to me. On June 14, 1988, Hannah was born. I was so happy to have a daughter. In the meantime, we were attending Travis Baptist in Memphis again for about a year. When he disagreed with the pastor or didn't feel like everything was going his way, we began home church again.

At one point when Hannah was a baby, I had enough of being beaten. I went to Robert Mack's parents and told them I had to take the kids and leave. They agreed. They could see Robert Mack was getting more violent with me particularly, but with the children also. He tended to use verbal abuse more toward the children. I tried to pack a lot of the clothes and hid them in the suitcases in the closet.

I made contact with Robert Mack's cousins Tom and Kathy in Crosbyton. They found a shelter for us. But, Robert Mack found out we were leaving. As we were finishing our preparations to leave, he drove up. I always thought his dad betrayed us. I'd experience much heartache because of Robert Mack, but this moment brought total devastation.

When Con became six years old, I was expected to home school. With the children so close together in age, they all learned together. I utilized the old time McGuffey Reader along with cassette tapes to teach phonics. No home school curriculum or support system existed. I found math materials and any other resource I could find in my limited amount of time. Their grandmother Martha helped me in the beginning, but her assistance faded eventually. I would set up a morning time for school to begin. Often Robert Mack interrupted late morning or noon to take the boys to work with him. The fact that my children learned is a miracle. With the lack of adequate materials, constant interruptions from Robert Mack requiring them to work, the pain I often suffered, and the numerous pregnancies, I marvel at the advancement in academics these children acquired. An innate intelligence was granted to each child no doubt. Thanks to God, they could grasp learning and could continue their education in a private church school after we began a new life.

Hannah was a toddler around one or two years old with the boys not far behind in age. While caring for four small children throughout the day, I canned vegetables as much as possible. He wanted me to sew a western shirt for him. I tried to explain time had not permitted me to sew, but he said I used the canning as an excuse not to sew. He sent me to sleep in the basement for a couple of nights, but that was better than sleeping outdoors. How I managed the care of four small children while sleeping in the basement, I don't know.

journal entry

I have had many hunks of skin pinched out of my side, back and the back of my neck and sometimes on the face. If he did happen to pinch my face or bruise me somewhere he thought people would see he would allow me to try and cover it up or we wouldn't go anywhere. And I better not ever tell or he would take me out and do away with me. They could do without me because he could hire someone to come in and do what I do. And they could do everything and it would be done right.

Back to the couple at Canyon where we had attended church. We drove over an hour to Canyon for church. He liked the husband because he tried to control his wife in the same way as Robert Mack. At least I could talk with his wife, someone who understood the situation. But, over time Robert Mack disagreed with the preacher in Canyon as well. We stopped going to church again. Church at home began. This brought me to the time of another pregnancy. I was pregnant with our 6th child, Noah.

Another couple started a church in their home. We drove 90 miles to their home for over a year. Then, of course, Robert crossed wires with the preacher from that home group. One more time he conducted home church. Eventually, we traveled to Crosbyton to attend church with Robert Mack's cousins. We began spending overnights with Tom and Kathy Taylor. That was great! Tom and Kathy were aware of many incidents within our home. I could talk with Kathy. Robert talked mainly with Tom's older brother Joe. Even if they argued, we still remained friends with Joe. My second miscarriage, which was my seventh pregnancy, occurred during this time. The longest period of years between children was three years because of the miscarriage.

CHAPTER FOUR

Robert joined the American Mountain Club.

Mountain Man

journal entry

I know there had to be so many times they would have liked to have run away from the house not the home. For they had no home. They feared the man with all of their being. The man was their Dad but only in name. There was no real bond except when he wanted a bond. I know people thought our children were really good and they were. The were just too scared to be anything but that. We all felt like when we were in a room with other people we had to look at him to see if we could breathe.

Backing up in time just a bit, Robert joined the American Mountain Club. With three young boys and Hannah just four months old, I was extremely busy. He bought an eighteen foot teepee so we could be active in the club. This may sound fun to some people but added extra difficulties for me. I sewed all our clothes, the covers for the bedrolls, and other covers we used.

When we reenacted the Fur Trade Era, we were expected to mimic the fur trading years of 1800 through 1853. I did all the cooking inside the teepee in cast iron skillets and kettles. Living inside the teepee had it's advantages as far as his actions toward me.

So many weeks at a time I dreaded him coming into the house. I feared his approach never knowing if a hit was coming my way or if he'd decided to spit in my face. I have mentioned he didn't allow me to clean my face. Sometimes that meant all day and all night.

He could be in a good humor one moment and become extremely angry in the next moment. If I said something he didn't like, he immediately turned against me. His fist hit my head, my face, or the middle of my back. Many nights he slugged me in the middle of my back and shoulders to the point of cracking a couple of ribs on each side of my shoulder blades. Some days the pain in my shoulders hurt so severely, I didn't know if I could make it through the day. No choice figured into the picture, because I had babies needing my care. Many times I took the slugs to protect the children asking that he hit me instead of them. He ended the beatings by saying none of this would happen if I were a submissive wife.

journal entry

I tried so hard to be loving, and show affection and sometimes it would calm and sometimes it wouldn't. He could hurt me so badly and I would be in so much pain. And night time would come and I dreaded that time so much. Cause you could never tell him no about sex. Didn't matter if you were on your cycle or if you were 9 months pregnant. And the past few years I felt like I was being raped when we had sex. And usually had to give in or I would be hit. I have been beaten in my shoulders so many times because I wanted to say no to sex. And sex was another thing I did wrong. It made him angry when someone bragged about something I did and not about him.

He would hit me on the back and kick me in the shins more than any other place. These places were covered up with the long dresses I was commanded to wear. With material covering most of my body, bruises were not visible.

I bought a splitter for the garden water faucet while he attended an American Mountain Man Reenactment. Since the hardware store carried plastic splitters only, that's what I bought. He wanted a brass splitter, so my purchase of a plastic one set him off. Without giving me a chance to explain, he took me to our bedroom and beat me with the belt he wore to the reenactments, which was over three inches wide. I had six or eight whelps across my bottom making it difficult to sit or sleep for weeks.

Sometimes I would have to sleep outside for weeks at a time.

29

journal entry

I have been locked out of my home more times than I can count. he would let me do all the household duties and then when it came night he would put me outside to sleep. Sometimes I would have to sleep outside for weeks at a time. Sometimes he would let me have some bedding to sleep on, and sometimes he wouldn't. This happened summer and winter to me. Not so bad in the summer, but in the winter it could be as cold as 20 degrees or colder. I might have my coat and nothing else to keep me warm. Even if he let me have a blanket, it would still be really cold and I wouldn't sleep much for I was so cold. I have sat on a plastic milk crate and leaned up against the house all night.

journal entry

He hit me on the left eye and made a pretty good slit that bled. I needed stitches. He hit me with a can of fire ant poison on the right side of the upper lip. I needed stitches but was not able to get them. The scar is still visible if not covered with make up. I couldn't wear make up then. He hit me over telling me I was not going to let me make hair bows for Hannah's hair. He had given me permission to buy the ribbon and make them at my cousin Karen Lynne's house. Then we got them made he said that he didn't say I could make them even though he knew my cousin knew the story. He said he hit me to show that I had not submitted to him and I was not a wife but a bitch and that's all I would ever be.

We started traveling to Rendezvous as part of the American Mountain Club. Hannah was only six months old when we participated in our first Rendezvous that included our entire family. I made all the clothes as usual including a parka for Robert Mack made from a Hudson Bay blanket. I did everything possible that was like the 1800's. When we got home I put away and washed everything. A few days later, Robert Mack became upset. He came inside and told me I didn't act right around all the other mountain reenactment men. He said I needed to learn a lesson. He laid into me with his fist banging my shoulder blades until I heard them crack. He kept hitting me. Only did he stop when we saw I needed to nurse Hannah. I could hardly hold my precious baby girl in my arms to let her nurse. Just functioning was painfully difficult for several weeks. But, I had no choice. He lived in a horrible mood almost every day.

journal entry

About 5 nights in a row he made me sleep outside with only a quilt and my coat. And on the 6th night I had enough and told him he was wrong to make me sleep outside. And he said he had every right to discipline any way the Lord told him to. And I said that was not coming from the Lord. The kids were already in their beds but probably not asleep. He grabbed me by the hair and drug me by the hair to the back door

Some of the men who were involved in the American Mountain Man Club exposed Robert Mack to more radical thinking. Their beliefs centered around citizen sovereignty. They did not believe in driver's licenses, insurance, social security cards, or paying taxes. He traveled to seminars learning ways to make these beliefs a reality. Then he began attending Bo Grits Survival Seminars. A local newspaper described the group. "The Idaho County auditor's office reported people filing documents declaring themselves "sovereign citizens," not beholden to the federal government."

Robert Mack and I attended two more Bo Grites Seminars. We learned more about survival and ways of getting out of being controlled by the government. Between 1991 and the beginning of 1992 I lost a baby at my parent's house. We were traveling back to Memphis from the seminar. Robert Mack knew I had some problems with bleeding. He tried to be so nice during the time I miscarried. But, he gave me one day to recuperate, and we left my parent's home. He never spoke to me on the trip home. When we arrived home, he told me for days I lost the baby because I was of the devil and a no good wife. He said I didn't want to submit and be the kind of Christian wife I should be. This kind of talk went on for months. He would come inside the house and say, "How's the slut doing?" He wouldn't speak to me for the rest of the night.

journal entry

Not sure when other people who were in our lives also came to the conclusion that they couldn't stand to be around Robert Mack. For he made every one so angry the last few years we were married. And this includes friends (the word "friends", I use lightly because I don't think Robert Mack ever had any friends), family, and people we dealt with whether it was someone we were buying something from, or people that were in his American Mountain Club to get out of all government things. All of these people soon came to the conclusion they hated Robert Mack or at least they didn't like anything he stood for.

None of his behavior ever affected his appetite for sex. I became pregnant with Micah. This period of time was my longest stretch without having a baby. I found a midwife and planned a home delivery. Our friends Shane and Janet told us about Leah Hernandez, who lived in Amarillo, had been a midwife for over sixteen years. She came to visit me. About the seventh month I began some spotting.

Robert Mack had been some nicer but not great. About a month before Micah was due, I hemorrhaged. Robert Mack rushed me to the hospital in Childress. After his birth, he was flown on care flight to the North West Texas Hospital neonatal ICU in Amarillo. I didn't stay in the hospital long. Robert Mack made sure the kids were all settled with his parents then drove back to Childress for me. We traveled back home to Memphis to grab some necessary items. I took a quick bath, and we headed to Amarillo. Robert Mack stayed a few days at the Ronald McDonald House with me. The first night he was actually nice. With no children needing my care, I enjoyed a leisurely bath. He thought I would never come out. Finally, I laid down in the bed, and he thought we should talk. His idea of a topic was to "talk about how things had to change in our marriage." The change was expected from me. I had to become a better wife and be more supportive in what he was trying to do about getting out of all the government stuff. He said, "You just want to get some sleep and rest." We had eaten before settling in at the Ronald McDonald House. I was so exhausted I didn't want to eat.

While he was kissing me good night he was trying to get close enough to have sex. He did force himself partially into me. I just said, "Please no." And, he said ok. But, the next day he acted mad all day. We stayed in the ICU all day except when doctors were making their rounds. I used a pump so they could give Micah my milk. After a couple of days, though, Robert Mack's parents called. They asked him to pick up the kids. Robert Mack went home. He and the kids drove to Amarillo the next day to see Micah and me. He acted fine until they started to head back to Memphis, then he said I was not acting right. He complained I wasn't talking to him right. He complained I didn't act like I was glad they had come.

He kept going over and over the recipe asking me how to cook biscuits. The kids said he burned them, but he said they were not crumbly biscuits like mine. He managed to pinch me in my side several times bringing blood and bruises which no one could see. They hurt terribly and became very sore. He took the children and left after supper at the Ronald McDonald House.

With the ongoing exhaustion, the difficult pregnancy, and Robert Mack's abuse, I'd had enough. When they were pulling out I told Robert Mack to go to hell. I didn't think he heard me, but he did. He circled and drove back to the front door of the Ronald McDonald House telling me he'd get Micah, but not me, the next day. The doctors were releasing Micah. I said I was sorry when he arrived back the next day. He acted like everything was fine, that nothing had taken place. I was still exhausted when we arrived home, but I knew all my duties were there waiting for me.

The children had tried their best to keep the house for Robert Mack. He had made them do nearly everything. Micah was settled, and I tried to get things back in order. That night supper ended without incident. I fed Micah and checked on everybody else. I went to bed early knowing I would feed Micah again in a few hours. Regular breast feeding was important in helping him gain more weight. He weighed 5 lbs. 3 oz. Robert Mack followed me to bed shortly thereafter. He wanted to make love, and I told him no. Of course, he didn't like that and he hit me in the back, pinched me and called me a slut and a bitch. He accused me of fooling around while I was staying at the Ronald McDonald House!

I tried to make him understand how exhausted I felt. He said a submissive wife wouldn't act like me and would meet her husband's needs.

journal entry

He tried to be nicer a few days after that because he needed to have his dad help him with some things by putting what we had left to farm in his dad's name. And we were running out of money and it had to be me to go and ask for the help of him signing the papers and asking for money. Robert Mack's daddy had to go to the bank and take out a loan to help us just to live. And this continued on like this for about a year maybe a little more.

journal entry

trip to Colorado - And when I couldn't tell him something on this trip he took my hand that had an apple core in it and slammed it flat against my ear and jaw. I had a huge bruise on the side of my face. And several times on the trip he would get mad and he would just spit all over my face. And did this a lot. And many times he would do this in front of the kids. And tell me I couldn't wipe off. And they need to know what a no good mother I was.

He would just spit all over my face.

On this same trip we went fishing. I cooked nearly everything on the whole trip. There was a few times when we were out sight seeing that he got mad and would make me get out of the vehicle and told me they were going to leave me there. Once he did drive off and then turned around and picked me up and told me to get in and would tell the children the reason he did that was to show them how I didn't submit to his authority like the Bible told me to. At this Colorado trip I was pregnant and several times he would hit me on the shoulder blades and bruise them badly. And then acted like when were out everything was fine.

During this same time period, I was banished once again to sleep outdoors. I resisted. He grabbed his 357 pistol and ordered me outdoors. I still resisted, so he caught my hair and dragged me to the door. I screamed to the top of my lungs, so he clamped his hand over my mouth. I bit down on his thumb as hard as possible. At that point, I didn't care that I hurt him. Breaking loose, I ran to his parent's house five blocks away. They couldn't seem to grasp what had happened not wanting to believe me. My thoughts flashed back to the children's safety, but I knew he was more interested in finding me. I knew, also, he was more interested in determining if a neighbor had heard me scream.

CHAPTER FIVE

Seeking Sovereign State

I experienced ongoing abuse for eighteen years; however, the children did not escape his madness.

journal entry

On Feb. 1998 he burned Caleb with a welding rod on the right arm because Caleb didn't plug in the light in the correct outlet. When I doctored the arm Robert Mack got mad at me. The children have been whipped with a horse bridle, fence rebar, boards with nails. Gideon was whipped with a wire brush ripping the flesh off his back. Con was buried in mud along the cow pond and left for 3 hours of more. Elijah in 1997 was hit with a crowbar and made to stand in the corner. Robert Mack poured gasoline on his back that made blisters. He said I couldn't wash it off but I did anyway. That night I slept outside and several nights after that. In the spring of 1997 Robert Mack picked up Noah and threw him against the side of the Suburban.

Many times I begged Robert Mack to hit me instead of the children. Many times I could talk him into that. Only if I could have saved them completely from being subjected to his uncommonly harsh treatment. Like my abuse, he'd try to hit them on the butt area or somewhere not visible. He'd whip them when I wasn't around so I couldn't take up for them. When I found out what he'd done to them and tell him he was wrong, he'd beat me.

journal entry

Robert Mack's dad finally figured he wasn't going to listen to any of us so he called Robert Mack's cousins Tom and Joe. They were at our house by breakfast to talk to him and he gave them the story of me being the not submissive wife and I had to be disciplined. They said he responded to them calmly. They came over to Robert Mack's parents and told me what was said but felt Robert Mack would not change. About 12, Robert Mack called, said to be out front if I want to come home and If I knew what was good for me, I would be out there waiting for him. I got home and he started calling me a slut, bitch, and a no good wife and mother and some other horrible words.

And told me that he was going to slit my throat and let the dogs lick up my blood. In fact later that day we were in the front yard and he was still going on about what I had done and he took the knife out of the case he carried on his belt and held it at my throat.

And when he did he cut my throat some to bring blood and he looked up and saw that our neighbor across the street was in the front yard. And Robert Mack dropped the knife into the grass and put his arms around me and told me to go into the house. He watched out the window for a long time. He didn't say anything the rest of the day. He made me sleep on the couch the next several days. But he was such a sex addict, he made up enough long enough to get what he wanted out of me and I would just lay there with no feelings whatsoever. And with tears running out of my eyes and being as silent as I could be.

Then came Enoch. We started out again with the same midwife. I did well physically this time except for the times Robert Mack became upset. He was attending the Take Texas Back meetings. Then, he was trying to convince me our Memphis life was coming to an end. I don't know how he found out about Marvin Skipper in Oklahoma. He had a building business including other kinds of work. Robert Mack talked back and forth with Marvin. We had no income at all. He made me ask his parents for money.

We drove to Crosbyton on Sundays, or we had home church. We were still trying to have a garden. The winter brought many hardships. Robert Mack either stayed in the bed all day or sat in his chair all day and stared at the floor. Sometimes he'd sit by our garden area on a crate and read hunting magazines. Sometimes he would talk to people on the phone about leaving the government's system. The midwife was still coming to the house to check on me. Toward the end of April everything I did or said made him mad. Losing everything was my fault. Losing the farm and getting speeding tickets were my fault. According to him, I didn't support him in all he was trying to do.

During the last couple of weeks of April I slept outside on the back porch. At least he let me have several blankets and a pillow this time. I was sleeping outside at nearly nine months pregnant. In the mornings I'd go inside and begin the multiple tasks of a homemaker. The hits I had suffered on my shoulder blades where the cracks occurred, were bruised and inflamed. Sleeping outside without much comfort increased the pain in my body. How can a man treat his wife, who is carrying his baby, so cruelly? I tried to tell Martha Lou and Robert what he was doing. They would say, "I don't know what's happened to Robert Mack. He's lost all his senses." And that's where it would end.

The morning I had Enoch was difficult for my water had broken late the day before. Leah came down from Amarillo and stayed the night. Early morning she gave me some Pitocin to speed up the delivery. Enoch was born before lunch. Martha Lou came over to take the children to their house. She didn't like the fact that the children were around when Enoch was born. What could I do about that? Leah thought Enoch was not breathing well enough, so an ambulance came from Childress. Robert Mack went in the ambulance. He acted like I was the love of his life. Leah cleaned everything up, changed and washed the sheets while I cleaned up. After I dressed, she took me to Childress.

The doctor still didn't like the sound of his lungs, so they flew him to Northwest Texas Hospital's neonatal ICU in Amarillo. Robert Mack and I went to Memphis to tell the children we were going to Amarillo. They stayed at their grandparent's home again. We got a room at the Ronald McDonald House but stayed at the hospital as long as possible. I sure needed rest, for I had endured childbirth and hadn't stopped for two days. I tried to rest. Robert Mack didn't say much, but began telling me how sorry he was for treating me badly. He said this over and over again. The next day he left for Memphis. Enoch stayed in the hospital for about a week. Home life was calm. It seemed to me like Robert Mack was working at being calm. When Enoch was about six months old, I broke my arm. As though the serious break weren't enough, I suffered other problems with my arm.

journal entry

We had come to my parent's home for a visit. The kids had new roller skates, and I thought I was still young. I put them on and in about 5 minutes, I fell and broke my right arm. The doctor could not put it in a cast because the bone would not stay stable. In surgery they drilled 3 places to attach pins. One hole was drilled on my hand below the index finger with 2 more places in the middle part of my forearm. A bar attached to the pins. Every few weeks we returned to Greenville so the doctor could adjust the bar. I did have the use of my fingers, and it's a good thing because all the garden vegetables needed attention. I canned and dried fruits and vegetables in the dehydrator. I cut up everything from beets, cucumbers, carrots to fruits. The freezer was filled with frozen vegetables and jars of jelly filled the shelves. I got to where I could knead bread and still baked 7 loaves of bread 3 times a week.

We made the trips to Greenville in one day. Six hundred miles is a long trip with a nursing baby. When Robert Mack became upset during this time, he'd say he wasn't taking me to the doctor. Twice when I was applying alcohol around the pins, he got mad about something and hit my arm causing the skin to pull away and bleed. I wore the bar for 11 1/2 weeks. My work continued as usual. Two babies were in diapers, and unless we were traveling, I used cloth diapers. Unless we had rain or snow, I had to hang them on the clothes line. A cast would have limited me to one arm, and everything would have taken much longer. The sleeping outside would have been more difficult if that's possible.

CHAPTER SIX

Broken Bow Failure

Robert Mack set up an interview with Marvin Skipper in Broken Bow, Oklahoma. They gave him a job. He had lost everything in Memphis connected with the farming business. This point in time found me pregnant again with baby Enoch only six months old. In Oklahoma, we moved our furniture into a house with no water. So, we actually stayed in a church on the property owned by the Skippers. Dorm rooms had been constructed inside the church. The three older boys moved tons of rocks to make way for a water line for the house. This large church had washers and dryers that were used for tent meetings two times a year. We were given permission to use them during that time, but at the end of a tent meeting someone disconnected them. After that, I rode to town a couple of times with Debbie Skipper's sister-in-law to a Laundromat. When this lady and her husband moved, I was left without transportation. Robert Mack would not take me into town to wash our clothes. He found a rub board and made me use the big sinks in the church to hand wash all the laundry. My hands looked like chopped meat.

Robert Mack thought he'd found a man who believed as he did. I suppose he did in some ways. They both tried to see how they could "outfox" the government. They worked at avoiding anything mandated by the government. They wanted to control everything. His job moved smoothly for a couple of months, then the situation slid downhill. Apparently Robert Mack made a pass at the boss's wife. That ended that.

They began by telling him they didn't have enough work for him. He worked only a few days a week for a time. Then, one day they actually fired him. He drove the family to Memphis where Robert Mack laid the groundwork to his parents about his job situation or lack of job situation. And, of course, the job loss was not Robert Mack's fault. I was told later he had forced himself on Marvin Skipper's wife almost to the point of rape.

Robert Mack loaded us in the Suburban so quickly, we left with very little. The people in Broken Bow called and said they were going to put all of our belongings outside and set them on fire. Robert Mack and the older boys loaded up a U-Haul. All I heard was how everything went wrong with poor Robert Mack. His dad put his name on the dotted line again and somehow found movers to take our furniture to a storage unit in Childress. We stayed at Robert's parents for almost a month. He didn't do anything for weeks. His Dad had created a storage building from a pick up bed with a camper attached. Robert Mack spent hours in their backyard in this makeshift storage shed. He sat and read magazines about survival and anti-government matters. He talked about how sick with depression he felt, making him unable to function. According to him, he couldn't look for a job because of the depression.

His Dad, whose health was not good, told him he had to make himself go out and find a job. I know his dad was tired of paying for everything, which had gone on for many, many years. I don't know how many times I asked for money, especially the last few years we lived in Memphis. Instead of facing his parents, he always forced me to ask. I know Robert L. took out several loans to help out Robert Mack. He could spin a good "feel sorry for me" tale. It's like he pushed a control button on his Dad. By the end of that month, Robert L. realized Robert Mack was not trying to get a job. He told him emphatically something would have to give. Robert Mack moved into action taking his resume to several places like health food stores in Amarillo and Dallas. No one cared to hire him with his uncut, untrimmed beard. He turned people off. They looked on him as untrustworthy.

After a month, we were in and out of his parent's home. He did prepare his resume. We drove to Amarillo, Lubbock, and Crosbyton looking for a job. Then we landed back in Memphis. Again his parents would say he really wasn't trying to find a job. He turned the blame to me. Soon he'd start calling me names like slut, no good, bitch and end by saying I was going to hell. He said if I had been a good submissive wife, we wouldn't have lost everything. All through the years he said I was unfaithful. I wonder when I could have found the time or the means of transportation to meet another man?

One day after we had stayed at his parent's house for months, his dad said we were leaving. He said we could live with my parents in Greenville for awhile. They had paid for all the food and everything else we needed. They realized, again, Robert Mack was not trying to find a job. But, Robert Mack made sure to tell me I wasn't doing my part by supporting him. He wasn't honest with his parents about job hunting, but they knew.

He arrived at a certain point where he spent long hours, especially at night ranting about how bad I was. He'd start hitting me in the back, pinching me, and spitting on me. He might act nicely for a few days to have sex with me. Yes, I became pregnant while in my parent's home. We figured the baby would be due about the first of November. From the beginning my pregnancy was not sound. Some spotting began, and I could predict something bad was going to happen. In no way could I stop the turn of events that lay ahead.

⤜⧼⧽⤛

CHAPTER SEVEN

Loss of Control

journal entry

By the beginning of April my Dad (Mr. Bevill) told Robert Mack he wasn't going to live off them either. He got a job at the Rubbermaid plant working at night. So that meant he would sleep from 7:30 a.m. until 5-6 p.m., then get up, eat, and spend most of the day sitting outside behind my Dad's storage building. And would complain off and on through the day the kids were too loud. My Dad told him he had better register our suburban and get his driver's license because there were so many cops on the way to the Rubbermaid plant and they would eventually stop him and give him a big ticket or haul him off to jail and he would not bail him out.

Basically at this point, my dad saved our lives. We had tried to find help for food, but because Robert Mack wouldn't let us have birth certificates and social security cards, we hit a dead end. Besides that, he said my "going to hell parents" weren't telling him what to do. On one occasion while in my parent's home, he said he ought to go and blow up his parent's house and then go to Idaho and do the same to his brother's house. After voicing this the first time, he said it many times. He also said they were all no good and stupid and didn't understand anything about the Word of God.

Sometime back in Oklahoma, he pulled a muscle that caused a hernia. When he'd been working for about a month at Rubbermaid, he hurt his arm. He tried to blame the hernia on the

Rubbermaid job as well. He lied so he could receive temporary Medicaid that would pay for the hernia repair surgery. He had the gall to call everyone in the world a liar. He also complained about his wrist being hurt on the job. They did actually pay for medical bills related to his wrist, but they would not pay for his hernia surgery.

Before he could return to work following the wrist episode, they called to dismiss him from the job. He tried to file unemployment, but because he was fired, he could not collect unemployment. In the meantime a record for an unpaid traffic ticket showed up. A Greenville policeman came to my parents home to serve him with a warrant. He would either pay up or serve time in jail. They came by the house several times before catching him. He decided rather than pay the fine he would spend time in the Memphis jail. He told me that he was going to take Caleb, our second oldest son, with him. Thank God the night before he left he changed his mind.

The Sunday before he went to Memphis we had home church. Ha! Ha! The whole speech had nothing to do with the Lord. It was all about staying on a long rope, which represented the family. The family was held together by just a thin piece of rope. Speaking to the boys, he said, "It's up to your no good Mother whether everything works out in our family. The reason everything bad has happened and what is happening now causing me to go back to Memphis is because of your no good Mother!"

He realized my parents would arrive home soon, so he stopped talking. My parents left again at 5:30 for Sunday night church. Robert Mack had evolved into a foul mood and hit me hard on the upper part of my left arm. He was wearing heavy lace up boots and kicked me up and down the front of my left shin. He made me wear long jumpers so no one could see the bruises. The next day I had a doctor's appointment to check on the child I had carried for four months. Spotting the whole time, I had many concerns.

After these appointments, we usually took the kids to Graham Park to give my parents a break. This particular day Robert Mack said we should take the kids back to my parents and go somewhere to talk. This was different for him. My insides told me something was different, and I really felt scared. When we arrived back to the house, my Uncle Odell was there. That made me feel good, and I went in the house. Mother was preparing tuna fish sandwiches with loads of good stuff in the tuna. Robert Mack came in and said we should leave. I said we couldn't because I needed to help my mother in the kitchen with the tuna salad. That made him angry.

Before we finished making the tuna sandwiches, my Aunt Faye and Uncle Monty came over. By the time we finished eating, it was getting late. He had taken the kids outside to eat instead of being in the house with all of us. He finally came in, sat down on the floor, and wouldn't talk to anyone except to stare harshly at me. Everyone went home. We got the kids to bed. He was so angry.

He clamped his hands around my throat trying to cut off my air. He voiced his usual statements about throwing me out a window with my throat cut and letting the dogs lick my blood up. He said everyone would know I was going to hell like my parents. Enoch, who was asleep in our room, made sounds so he stopped for awhile. We went to bed, and I slept as far to the edge as possible. That was my only way of saying I was hurt. But, before I could get to sleep, he hit me in the back and said I had never been a good wife or mother. I was nothing but a slut and a bitch.

Robert Mack was forced to register the Suburban, obtain insurance, and pay for a car inspection. Otherwise, he would be caught eventually. His driver's license required renewing. He had given the car title to former friend Larry Hickam, so the car would not be in his name. Now, Robert Mack needed it back to register the car. Eventually, Robert Mack finished with these necessities of life, which we should have had anyway. Each day he became angrier with my parents and me. Daddy said Robert Mack should get some help from Human Resources for food. We had no birth certificates thanks to Robert Mack. Of course, birth certificates and Social Security cards were required as part of the process for obtaining Medicaid. He tried to file unemployment about this time, but Rubbermaid had fired him. He couldn't collect unemployment. For a few weeks after that job collapsed, he had my parents believing he would be going back to work.

He did get the paper work started so he could get medical Medicaid for a short time to cover his hernia surgery. And, he completed the paperwork Medicaid required related to my pregnancy.

The next morning Daddy and Mother cooked breakfast as always. I followed him back to the bedroom after breakfast. He sat on the bed and ask me to sit beside him. "I'm not taking Caleb with me." My heart leaped with joy. He'd decided he shouldn't return since all of us "would be better off without me." I tried to stay calm. Trying to act loving, I assured him everything would get better. We would just need to have faith. But, he said he would never see the new baby, he would never see the new baby.....repeatedly. Never did he shed one tear as he spoke. He hugged the children and me goodbye. I knew even though he said he would never see us again, he wasn't telling the truth. Knowing this down deep in my bones, I moved into action to save myself and my children.

❧❧

CHAPTER EIGHT

Call to Action
and Secret Revealed

journal entry

Not sure when the love I once had for Robert Mack turned into literal hate. Never thought I could do harm to him. Just prayed continually the Lord would change him, take him away from us, or change me so that I wouldn't make him so angry.

The morning he left for Memphis, he acted so sorry for his actions and so nice. Of course, he wanted sex. I told him no because of the blood spotting. Such relief I felt when he left me alone. We ate breakfast, and finally he left at 11 a. m. I felt relief again. He hugged everyone, but the children made no real effort to tell him goodbye.

Thirty minutes after he left, I flooded the commode with big clots of blood. For some time, I was unable to alert anyone. When I could leave the bathroom, I found Con and my dad. I just lost it and couldn't stop crying. They both held me, which seemed like forever. In a matter of moments, the relationship with my oldest son changed. He realized from that point on, for whatever laid ahead of us, he knew and I knew he had committed himself to help me.

A policeman from Greenville came and took my statement about loosing the baby the day Robert Mack left. How the abuse, the beating Robert Mack did to me before he left was the reason I lost the baby. He had beaten me several times, while I was pregnant, when we stayed with my parents. But, as always, he hit me where the bruises would not show.

The next day Shirley Keath, the next door neighbor, took me to a lady doctor. Since Shirley worked at the hospital, she had contacts for immediate help. The doctor wanted Aunt Laura Faye to see all of the bruising on my legs and arms. Robert Mack had kicked me on the front of my right and left front shins. My right arm from the top down of my elbow was bruised badly, also. The doctor was shocked that something worse had not happened to me. She understood Robert Mack was a dangerous man.

After confirming the baby was dead, they performed a D&C to remove the tissue and blood. By late evening I had survived the day's ordeals and found rest at my parent's home again. Aunt Laura Faye and Shirley stayed close. They knew Robert Mack had supposedly left, but they didn't trust him. He could have turned around and come back to town.

Even though my physical body had suffered a catastrophe, my emotions were drained; my spiritual self overcame the other damaged parts of me. The sense of survival demanded that I act and act quickly. Armed with the continuing strength only the Lord Jesus Christ could have supplied me all those years, I sprang into action the very next day. My Aunt Laura Faye took me to Women In Need, a housing facility for battered women and children. We began the paperwork to obtain a protective order. The first step was referred to a "no trespass order" making my parent's home off limits for Robert Mack. The order set a distance of no closer than 500 feet should he appear in the neighborhood

During this time he was extremely angry over the no trespassing notice. Now, I was working on obtaining a Protective Order as well. Sherry Sheffield became my knight in shining armor. She knew her business. She knew how to help someone in desperate need and in horrible situations. Her job didn't fit into the 8 a.m. to 5 p.m. window, for she cared about the women who walked into the doors of WIN (Women in Need). She understood women who entered her door had arrived at the end of their road. I bonded with her as a friend and ally. We have stayed in touch through the years. We spent days and days going through the information she needed and completing paper work. From the beginning I knew she believed me. She worked with all her might to get the Protective Order ready.

Judge Leonard granted the protective order. Protective orders are effective for only one year, then all the paper work must be filed again. On the 7th of July the procedures for the divorce began. This gigantic step would make Robert Mack angry. He didn't come to court the day the judge granted the protective order. Robert Mack's lawyer tried to make contact with him to no avail. He later said he had faxed his lawyer stating he wouldn't appear in court because of his surgery. Neither his lawyer nor the court ever received a fax stating that fact. But, the judge granted the protective order anyway.

Because of the severity of the case, the judge didn't grant a continuance. After he granted the judgment, the judge called me to the bench, "Mrs. Moss, you know that this is only a piece of paper. I suggest you get something to protect yourself and your children, because this man will hurt you." In fact, Robert Mack broke the protective order several times. We called the police each time. I never came face to face with Robert Mack that day and prayed I never would. I needed rest desperately because of the continuing emotional process of our urgent situation.

Uncle Odell helped me buy a pistol for protection. When I got it I slept with it under my pillow every night. We put the chest of drawers in front of the bedroom windows in case Robert Mack tried to break in the house. On this day we tried to stick really close to the house for I knew Robert Mack was suppose to be in Greenville for his check up following surgery.

Uncle Monty took Con with him to work. I had a hard time trying to keep the other children quiet and mind me. I didn't want to upset Mother and Daddy any more than necessary. I tried to pray and understand why my children weren't minding very well. All the while I knew it was because their lives had been turned upside down. Even though they were trying to understand and some things they did understand, this situation was very hard on them. I couldn't expect children to be adults. Mother and Daddy's next door neighbors brought food and tried to ease the burden.

Aunt Laura Faye and I went to see Holly Gotcher, an attorney, to explain the situation and request her help. We hoped she would take my case pro bono. At first she said no, but later she changed her mind.

She explained she couldn't sleep after turning me down. I signed papers to file for divorce. Thankfully, I hid money for the cost of an attorney, but she took my case pro bono.

While he was gone back to Oklahoma to retrieve our furniture, he drove to Childress to the storage unit, picked out some of his guns and ammunition, and took them to Dallas for a Gun and Knife Show. Since he didn't have a key to the storage unit, he cut off the lock and replaced it with another lock. He also sold guns in order to hire a lawyer. His first lawyer checked him out and apparently dropped him as a client.

Today, the first day of July, Aunt Laura Faye drove me to the Texas Department of Human Resources. We had a 7:30 a.m. appointment. Con returned at 12:30 to pick up our paperwork enabling us to acquire a Lone Star Food Card. All during this time, we were on guard watching for Robert Mack to show up and do something to us. Also, paperwork for child support was underway. As we completed each step, I could imagine the anger erupting from him. But, I had to remind myself that every step lead us to freedom.

journal entry

And at this point his parents were as angry with me as Robert Mack. And they were in complete denial that everything through the years had not been so bad. And that Robert Mack could never be a dangerous man. And I know that he was their son, but how could they have forgotten all the breaks and bruises, the beatings with the belt and they knew all the times I was sleeping outside. And my heart broke so badly at this point. For I know now that I feel that I had lied all these 19 years about everything that Robert Mack had done to me and the children. And tried to convince the older ones that Robert Mack had not done all the horrible things that I had been written up in the protective order. And even though I forgave them for not believing me there will always be a little piece of my heart that will be broken because they didn't believe me. And that part I may never forget but I have been forgiven.

From the day that Robert Mack left, I did not speak another word to him. He called, and we would hang up the phone. With the protective order finished and in force, he had to be served. He drove to Crosbyton where his cousins lived to plead his case with them. His cousins had lost faith in him and believed nothing he said. They had determined not to fall into his control.

He drove to Benbrook near Fort Worth for empathy. He thought this friend held the same beliefs about women and family. He talked his friend into taking him to Greenville hospital for hernia repair surgery. I am positive the Lord guided my thinking. I knew he had gone to Memphis, Crosbyton, or possibly Benbrook. I had already gone to bed with so many thoughts running through my mind.

A thought popped into my brain. Because the Medicaid for his surgery was valid for a short term, he would schedule that surgery very soon. The next morning I called Sherry Sheffield first to share the idea. Then I called the doctor's office to inquire about his surgery. He was in surgery! I hung up and called Sherry Sheffield back. Sherry sprang into action. When Robert Mack left recovery, the Deputy and the Sherriff served him the papers for the Protective Order. Later, the friend who came to Robert Mack's rescue said he had never heard a man say such horrible things.

As soon as Robert Mack had a chance, he tried to call and talk to me. My daddy said he tried to come across as being so sorry for all the things he had done to me and the children. We all knew he never meant it.

I took a letter Gideon got from his Grandmother Moss to Sherry Sheffield. She had sent him a birthday card with the letter enclosed. Basically, she wrote that everything his mother said was a lie. Gideon knew better.

Robert Mack stayed with his friend Lonnie and wife after surgery. But, Lonnie's wife told her husband she wanted him out as soon as possible. Robert Mack obtained another lawyer. Lonnie had driven him to Greenville for he couldn't drive after the surgery. Uncle Odell just happened to cross paths with Robert Mack in the same building. My uncle noticed Lonnie standing near his pick up. When they drove away, Uncle Odell tried to follow but soon lost sight of them.

By attending several gun shows, he had sold many of his guns and ammo. I thought he would never part with them. He knew he needed money, and selling his prized possessions was his only avenue for funds. The Protective Order stated his wrongdoings clearly, yet what had taken place while we were married was massive compared to information in the Protective Order. Robert Mack broke the Protective Order several times within the first two weeks. After he returned to his parent's house, they began calling. I wouldn't talk to him. I never spoke another word to him from the day he left my parent's home.

On one of the occasions he broke the Protective Order, he watched Gideon and Elijah dig a hole for a dug-out house in the backyard. As the boys were finishing their project, Gideon left the yard to pick up a tin metal piece for the roof. When he topped a rise behind the yard, his Dad was standing about 20 feet away from him. Robert Mack tried to talk with Gideon, but he began screaming for Elijah to run for the house. Realizing his dad was walking toward the house, Gideon screamed to the top of his lungs as he ran. The police arrived about five minutes after we called, but they could not find him. He had driven his Dad's red pickup back to Dallas.

While in the process of obtaining the Protective Order, Robert Mack called David and JoAnne Shirey, our church friends from Greenville, from back in 1980. They attended Ridgecrest Baptist Church where we attended at the time. Robert Mack met with David several times telling him about me. Even though Robert Mack told him I caused everything bad in the marriage, David read right through Robert Mack. He perceived him as a verbal, physical, mental, spiritual, emotional abuser to me and the children. To David's credit, he spent many hours talking with Robert Mack that the treatment toward his wife and family he called discipline was not from God.

Joanna related after the fact how Robert Mack tried to convince David that his actions were Biblical and from God. David clearly declared that when a person loves his family, he does not treat them unkindly.

He sent Gideon a birthday card and Hannah a flower plant on her birthday. Hannah let the plant die. His orders stated no contact at all. So, his parents started calling me and especially wanted contact with the children. The one time his parents talked to Con, they tried to defend Robert Mack by saying he would never hurt any of us. His parents knew differently in their hearts. They had seen the results of physical abuse and even witnessed him beating me to a pulp on my seat. At one time, they promised to testify against him. When I needed action from them, they turned against me.

As the oldest grandson, Con was more torn about talking with his grandparents. He wanted their support for his mother, but they supported his dad, their son. In fact, "His mother was in the wrong," a statement made to Con over the phone. Truly, I don't feel they thought I was in the wrong, but thought they had to stand up for Robert Mack. They had seen evidence of abuse through the years. They knew the fear he instilled in his family.

journal entry

The fear grew with each passing year. Fear and control was all that Robert Mack had for the last few years and for sure these last few weeks of me standing up to him for the first time in our whole marriage. And he was unable to use the control and fear on me right now. So he was having to resort to the help of his parents. And play on their sympathy and love he knew they had for him. But he knew that I was tying his hands where he had no options. For awhile he tried to convince me that he would fight me every step of the way and he would never give up his children. But the true hate for me was really coming out. I knew for a long time that there was no love for me and maybe down deep inside him some where he knew that I had had enough of his control and fear. He never thought I would take action to get out of the fear and control that he held over me and the children.

Robert Mack sent me a long letter explaining how sorry he felt about loosing the baby. But, as always, he faulted me. He envisioned me as unfaithful, when in actuality he had been unfaithful numerous times. The boys were with him on one of these occasions.

Then they were upset about Robert Mack's clothes. I boxed up and mailed them to Memphis. Since he didn't provide for his family, none of us had good clothing. Apparently, Robert Mack was pretty kind to his parents the last few weeks he was alive.

The younger children stayed close to my parent's house. Herman came by for Caleb and Gideon about 2 p.m. to help with Aunt Laura Faye's business. Con got home about 30 minutes later. He worked with Uncle Monty hanging gates at the Greenville high school. Working helped calm his nerves. Caleb and Gideon saw their dad at the corner of Sayle and Austin one day as my aunt was bringing them home. They ran in the house, locked the garage, and all the doors. The boys were really scared about him following them. When they were all at the house, we mostly stayed inside. We closed the garage door before dark and locked all the doors. Living like that was hard on us, but we had no choice.

On July 12, I called the police about 5 pm. Robert Mack was sighted up the street parked at a neighbor's home. They recognized him and called me. He had broken the protective order and began to stalk us.

The next evening Caleb had been disobeying me and picking on the other children. I sent him back to his bedroom to read his Bible. Soon, I followed to ask him what was going on with him. We read the Bible together for a few minutes. I remembered a special poem and began reading "Footprints in the Sand" to him. Before I finished ready, he began crying hard and shaking. Some time passed before he settled down. More time passed before Caleb could share a huge burden he'd been carrying on his shoulders for years. The words finally flowed out. Since his seventh year of life, his Dad had sexually abused him. For about 6 years this child of mine had dealt with horror. Robert Mack had forced him to look at pornography and commanded him watch his Dad with another woman at our own home in Memphis. This scene took place in our bedroom. He threatened him with knives and even with a gun a few times.

The threats continued the entire time of his abuse. Caleb knew at that moment that I believed him, and I would always believe him.

On July the 8th, 1998, we related Caleb's story to Sherry Sheffield at Women In Need. She contacted CPS, told him the story, and took paperwork to the police so they could arrest Robert Mack and put him away in jail. We actually drove to the CPS office. One of the boys thought he spotted the red pick up. We didn't park at the CPS parking area. Instead, we parked at the Herald Banner Newspaper office parking lot and walked to the CPS office. Watching with every step we took, we knew he could be anywhere for our neighbor's had spotted him earlier that day.

When Caleb finished telling his story of perpetual abuse for over six years, he was like a new boy. As we left the building, Caleb thought he saw the red pick-up. He was correct.

Finally, Robert Mack returned to Memphis, Texas, after his attempts to see and talk with us failed. However, we didn't really know his location and continued our apprehensive watchfulness. Robert Mack did ask his cousin Joe Taylor to talk with us, but Joe knew Robert Mack and his capabilities to harm us. His parents did continue to call speaking with Con several times.

I received a 7-1/2 page handwritten letter from Robert Mack dated June 13th. He asked me to forgive him five times. He said he had repented, changed, and had more understanding. Any trust I had in Robert Mack had died many years before. I couldn't imagine what he would put me through once he had me alone again. My duty to him was one of a "brood mare." He clearly lacked empathy or sympathy as he never realized the strain on my body from 11 pregnancies. His idea of the wife as an nonentity comes through in this letter:

"Con, Caleb, Gideon, Hannah, Elijah, Noah, Micah, and Enoch are my children, and they were given life by God Almighty and God has ordained that I should raise them for him and his glory and this can never be changed."

He went on to mention his faithfulness to me and the children, which of course, was not true.

On July 16th, Robert Mack talked with my mother and dad's minister. He wanted him to act as mediator for me and Robert Mack. A little humor enters my mind as I think about this. I knew he was desperate, because he hated anyone who was a member of the Church of Christ!

⚒⚒

CHAPTER NINE

Unexpected Release

The day Robert Mack took his life in 1998, the sheriff of Memphis served him with the arrest warrant for sexual abuse perpetrated against his son Caleb. Maybe because of the small town dynamic, he was granted permission by the sheriff to inform his parents first. The sheriff agreed to give him time for his mother to arrive home from church. From that point, he knew he could no longer fight me. He figured a way to still be in control, at lest in his mind. He found a picture of the children and hung it on the storage building in his parent's backyard. In front of the storage building a large tree stump from a tree cut down years before remained intact. He sat down on the stump, held his Colt revolver to his head, and took his life. Apparently, no one heard the shot.

When his mother came home from church, she changed her clothes as usual. After preparing lunch, she asked her husband if he had seen Robert Mack. Robert, still in bed because of poor health, said he had not and suggested she look in the backyard where he spent the majority of his time. His mother opened the back door and entered the yard calling him to lunch. Then, she saw him on the ground. She walked toward him and realized what had happened. In shock, I'm sure, she stopped abruptly. His brains were scattered all over the fence.

journal entry

But nothing could take away the joy from the facts that were told to me - that they served the warrant for his arrest the Sunday morning that he committed suicide.

The boys had gone to the deer lease for the weekend. After they arrived home about 2 p.m., I laid down to take a nap. From worrying and wondering about Robert Mack's location, I really couldn't sleep. I heard the phone ring.

I did cry some after hearing the news but not from sadness. Relief from fear brought with it a release of emotions. I can't remember the conversation with Martha Lou in detail. She wanted to know when I would be coming to Memphis. Robert Mack had the Suburban. I was totally dependent on my aunt and uncle for transportation, and they couldn't leave their business without making arrangements. She mentioned burial clothes were needed for Robert Mack. I had no car and eight children as my responsibility to ready for a life changing event. We managed to leave early the next morning arriving in Memphis by late afternoon. Thankfully, my aunt and uncle offered to drive us in their van. Robert Mack's parents, clearly upset about the trauma inflicted on them, blamed me for his death.

journal entry

Shortly thereafter, Con came into my room and told me Robert Mack had shot himself. His mother found him in the backyard before lunch. I found out that morning the Memphis Sheriff had served him with an arrest warrant for the sexual abuse to Caleb. As hard as everything was when we went back to Memphis, I knew days would improve. Anger was shown toward me because Robert Mack's parents and brother blamed me for everything. At the time, they couldn't realize I was tired of fighting for my life and didn't want to fear for my children any longer. There would be many trials ahead for us. Robert Mack's parents and I did resolve our differences before his dad died a year later. It took Jerry longer to come to grips with what Robert Mack had done to us even though I had shared with him a lot of what Robert Mack had done to me through the years. Joe Taylor and Tom and Kathy Taylor finally got through to Jerry how bad it was for me and the children. Jerry sent Caleb a card telling him that he believed him about the sexual abuse. There is a small part of Caleb that feels Jerry still doesn't believe him.

Con had not a tear in his eyes as he delivered the news that day. None of the children made any kind of a response much at all. I cried, but my tears were tears of relief. My children's faces showed that look as well. That night before Gideon went to bed, he told my dad he could finally sleep. For so many years he slept in intense fear.

We drove directly to a motel and checked in before going to the funeral home. There is no way I can describe the look on the children's faces when they saw their Papa in that casket. Their faces showed little emotion, rather a look of relief knowing they could breathe for the first time ever. They were calm and didn't shed one tear. Con might have cried some the day of the funeral. What we saw lying in the casket looked pitiful. Somehow they had fixed his face enough to have open casket. His eyelids were sown shut. His face so distorted from the shooting, but somehow he still had that angry, controlling face, almost like he was saying he had the last word.

I laid my hand on his chest and just stood there for awhile thinking, "Robert Mack, why did you have to be the way you were to me and the children?" It still didn't seem real to me even though I was standing there looking at his body. I had to look and feel the thumb I bit and brought blood. A deep scar remained. My memory brought the horrifying scene of his hand over my mouth and a 357 Magnum pistol at my head with his other hand. His words ran through my mind. "You are sleeping outside even if I have to shoot you and leave you outside to die so the dogs can eat you. You are nothing more than a no good slut and bitch. You've never been a wife or mother."

journal entry

They had to sew his eye lids together because he put the gun to his temple and it blew everything out on the fence that was in the backyard. None of his children said anything that I remember. The only thing I remember really doing is checking for the scar on his left hand down by his thumb. It was a scar that I had put there.

Arriving at the Moss' home was like walking into a room full of ice. I was the villain. His parents were so angry; I tried not to get upset. That was truly hard. They decided not to remember anything I suffered. They tried to separate the older children away from me to tell them how much Robert Mack (their papa) loved them. According to them, all he talked about the last days was a chance to see his family and make things right. They knew differently. They had suffered physical abuse from this man and were tired of witnessing or seeing the results of my abuse. Almost in the same breath, his parents said they couldn't make arrangements without me and why didn't I come the day before. One more guilt trip for me. Immediately, I thought of Tom Taylor, Robert Mack's cousin. I called Tom hoping he would conduct the service. He graciously accepted.

We didn't stay long at the Moss' home for Micah and Enoch were tired. After all, they were only two and four years old. Uncle Monty took Micah and the boys to swim in the motel swimming pool. When I got Enoch to sleep, I brought Micah in for bed. Even though I felt physically exhausted and emotionally drained, I slept very little.

Facing the next day with little sleep was difficult. Jerry Moss, his brother, blamed me for Robert Mack's death, too. Whatever they thought, I knew he had things I needed like the money from selling guns. I had to pay for his casket from those funds.

journal entry

They too knew that Robert Mack had said all those things before. But he never changed. He just said those things long enough to get us back. So he could have us fear him and he would have control over us. Robert and Martha Lou now said he wanted us all together. How could I or the children ever think their Papa would hurt me or them? What a laugh! Not like a funny laugh, but how could they say something like that and believe it. For they had seen how Robert Mack had hurt me physically for many years and he hurt he had done to the older children. They had told me and the children many times that they knew we were afraid of Robert Mack.

And we knew that Robert Mack was capable of being out of control. So for them to say that they couldn't figure out why we would not talk to Robert Mack or try to get together with him to work it out so we could be a family. And to know that he would never hurt was just unreal for me. And if looks could have killed me that day they would have done me in!

Along with conducting the funeral service, Tom sang with his wife Kathy. Since they are Primitive Baptists, all songs were sung accapella. This upset Robert Mack's mother and brother. But, oh well! Only a few friends of the family and very few family members attended the funeral home service. Some of Robert Mack's aunts, uncles, and cousins attended. My Aunt Patsy and Uncle Mack traveled from Gruver. My brothers came to support me.

journal entry

I don't think the day of the funeral me or the children shed a tear. I think I know since then they have. I had to grieve in my own way and they had to grieve in their way. Some of the grieving was through anger with me, which took years for us to work through. But, through the help of God, family, church, and counseling, we tackled the days that laid ahead. I tried so hard to help the children understand their dad's death was not their fault.

Members of the First Baptist Church prepared a meal for the family. Even though I appreciated the meal, I had already vowed not to step foot in another Baptist Church for worship. Now I could worship as I believed. I would never be controlled like that again! While we returned to the Moss's home again, Tom checked the Suburban for travel. The air conditioner didn't work, but at least we had transportation.

Before leaving, Uncle Odell, Uncle Monty, and my brother Jerry, loaded guns and ammunition in Uncle Odell's van. Robert Mack had stored unsold guns and ammo in his dad's shed.

Back at his parent's home, we said our good-byes. They thought we should have stayed longer but we couldn't and wouldn't at the time. Back in Greenville we sold several guns with the ammunition leaving some ammo the boys could use later for hunting. For months we rarely spoke with his parents. Now that I look back, maybe we should have stayed longer after the funeral. His dad died only a year after Robert Mack's death. Thankfully, some mending had taken place before Robert's death.

CHAPTER TEN

Journey of Hope

journal entry

My biggest regret is my children had to go through all of my torment from him and all of the torment that he did to them. And Robert Mack telling them that bad things happen to them, to me, and all the bad things that happened to Robert Mack was because of me. Because of me, meant that I was not submissive to him as a Christian wife. And that I wasn't a Christian so I couldn't be submissive, he would tell me. And since I wasn't a Christian, I was a child of Satan's. And I would always be going to hell. And I will always be a slut, and bitch forever.

We lived with my parents another year, then I began searching for a house. I had liquidated some coins of Robert Mack's he had evidently forgotten. With that money and some cash from Martha and Robert, a down payment became reality. By then his parent's anger toward me had changed. We loaded our furniture and boxes from storage and moved into our house. Having our own home was a giant step.

Several months passed then Grandpa Moss passed away. We made another trip to Memphis. After the funeral, we visited Tom and Kathy for a few days. The kids loved going to their home for they lived on a large ranch where Tom was foreman. Kathy made a revealing statement about my kids. She said this was the first time she'd ever heard all my children laugh.

How sad for them but how glad for them I felt. They could be themselves, laugh, and truly have fun. I talked to Tom, Kathy and Joe for hours, opening up and sharing what had been weighing me down for many years. All my heartaches emotionally and spiritually as well as the physical abuse had been bottled up. Only by God's grace did I not explode. They were greatly disturbed when I told them what Robert Mack had done to Caleb. We tried to analyze the why's of his sexual abuse toward Caleb. Robert Mack had a cousin who was involved in this way. He had been involved with pornography as well. But, the sexual abuse to his child caught up with him. Robert Mack and his cousin shared a common thread in that they both hated their Grandpa Moss, and he has been dead for many years. Apparently, they had even talked about how they couldn't stand the man. So, I can't know absolutely, but feel sure Grandpa Moss molested both of them. Perhaps this experience started the uncontrollable anger inside Robert Mack. The last few years he could never have enough sex to fill the void missing in his life.

Months passed and Uncle Jerry wouldn't have much to say to us. Only after a few years later did Tom, Kathy and Joe have a chance to talk with him about Robert Mack. They presented the real man that made up his brother. At that point his attitude became better toward us. But even now, Caleb feels a distance between himself and his uncle. Even though the uncle knows the truth, the barrier remains.

I'm often asked the question, "How could you have stayed in such a horrible situation?" From the moment we married, he began controlling my mind. His mind was set on what he wanted me to become. Maybe the reason Robert Mack waited so late in life to marry was to have a better chance at dominance. I was 11 years younger. I feared him from the beginning and believed his threats.

journal entry

I never remember feeling safe in my own house. Tried to make sure my children were safe and loved. Even though when they were with their Dad without me, they didn't always feel that way. I have two young sons who don't even remember their Dad. The older boys tell them some things. It's hard to feel they ever had a Dad. I don't have many things that even remind them of their Dad.

With each passing child and each passing year he became more and more controlling and more abusive to me, the children, his parents, my parents, family members, and other people that he thought were his friends. But, with each passing year these people avoided him. Every conversation led to topics where he was right and they were wrong. He told people they didn't know what they were talking about.

When he went into depression, I believe life faded for him. All through the years he controlled me, and he controlled the children. By "beating" the government and its bureaucracy, he controlled government. But, when his family needed the government for Social Security and Medicaid, he could no longer control his disengagement from government. He could no longer provide for his family and maintain his position of head of the house, so he lost his control over the family.

From living with the cruelty for so many years, I believe he was "eaten up" with Satan. No matter how much he read his Bible, quoted scripture, and prayed, all was used as a display to solidified his reason for control of his wife and family. How could God hear the prayers of a man who beat his wife and children, sexually abused a son, sought out pornography, and committed adultery? His prayers weren't prayers of repentance, for he considered himself in the right always.

journal entry

There were a few people I could share with some but never anyone that I could be completely honest with on how bad everything was with me and the children. One aunt on Robert Mack's side. His Aunt Rachel was a wonderful Christian woman who truly understood all that was going on with me. And was a true encourager. Not only in the words that she spoke to me but in the way she lived her life by the encouraging words she said to me. She truly meant the words that she quoted from God's Word. And I know she prayed for our family all the time. Joe Taylor was another that could listen to me and I knew he understood the hurt that the children and I were going through.

journal entry

I pray daily that people who are going through being hurt by a husband, a family member, or by anyone they will find a way to get out and can be healed and find peace. When things get so bad you think you can't continue that's when I pray that these people can have a personal relationship with the Lord. Hopefully they can have someone they can go to and share all with them. For they need someone so they can survive. I know that today I am having to deal with the physical person that did all the things to us. We are still dealing with the scars but they have dimmed with time. I feel my children have dealt with all that happened to us better than me. I still have to pick myself up from all that happened to us.

journal entry

My children looked to me for guidance through all that happened, through all the bad years and now through all the times now. And everything is not always easy. But I feel that we are all happy. We have a strong family relationship with each other. I know when something is going on with each of us we all care, good or bad.

The older boys have gone through the most of all the children. When we were here in our own house at the beginning I know the 3 older boys had it tough. They each seemed to be a loner. It took them awhile to get close.

We go through each day and we feel we have come so far and we have so many blessings. We still want life to be better for their children. I am not talking about money. It has weighed on me so much even now that my children's problems may have been my fault because I didn't get them out of our bad situation.

I think I'm making new strides in my life, then something creeps back to remind me of my old life. Physical pains from the abuse of my back and shoulders cause discomfort. The emotional abuse creeps back to cause deep heartache. People and books I read advise me to push on. Sometimes I just feel too plain tired from the pushing through I've already done while living inside the situation.

journal entry

    Caleb came by today. He asked me how the book was going. I said I was trying to work on it each day. For some reason he told me about this particular thing his dad had done to me that had stayed in his memory. He was probably 6 or 7. We were at my parents home. Robert Mack decided we would drive down to the Lake of the Pines where we went for our honeymoon. So we went to find the motel. Come to find out several years before there had been a fire and most of it burned down. Robert Mack decided to dig up a rose bush that was in front of our room where we stayed. He put it in a 5 gallon bucket he had in the back of the pick up. He did plant it in a flower bed at our home.

    When we left the lake we were doing some driving around and Robert Mack wanted to tell him something now to get some place by reading a map. This is one thing that would make him angry in a flash. He missed a turn because I wasn't telling him quick enough. He took a full cup of coffee and poured it all down the front of my shirt. It made a couple of blisters. So he said if you didn't have the devil in you I could read a map and be the person I should be. Caleb said he would never forget that. Shortly after this is when he started the sexual abuse to Caleb.

The smell of tomatoes in a greenhouse brought back the past today. Robert Mack worked in the garden but never as much as me and the children as soon as they were old enough. Many nights he pushed me out to either sleep in the garden or outside the back door. A smell, a word, an event, or even a dream can take my body back into the moment of being controlled by someone I literally came to hate. How thankful I am to God for bringing me to the point of forgiving him. But, memory brings back a moment causing a slight flicker or burning sensation in my soul. Healing comes with time, but some parts of the healing take longer than others.

journal entry

I have had someone come into my life who was not expected. Someone completely different as far as the way I am being treated. In this relationship I have peace when I am with this person. When I am away I seem to doubt myself. The doubts come when this voice comes to me and throws doubts that I have no worth as a person. I have made new friends in the past months and they bring excitement to me. Almost in the same breath the doubts will come flying in with a vengeance. And all over again I am not in control. And I look at the new relationships I have and friends and wonder how they could like a person like me. I even wonder how my children have confidence in me as a mother. Am I helpful to them? Have I really done all that I should to be there for them? Where and how does a person put a stop to the voice of someone who has hurt you so deeply? Even in writing these words it's like the sound of a thundering voice telling me I am not capable of doing this book. There is no self-worth inside me. It is really hard to make myself read back over what I have written. Because I get to thinking I'm not capable of any writing. Sometimes I can feel so strong and I know I have made some giant steps. I know I have grown in my relationship with my children and my Lord. Never again do I want to have the feeling I am losing either one. I have tried to come to the point of having no doubts and have forgiven the one who has hurt me beyond measure physically, mentally, and spiritually.

Since the death of my husband and father to my children, July 19,1998, I still question so many things.

journal entry

Everyday my life seems to be a new adventure. A day of deciding whether I am in control or I'm letting Robert and Satan be in control. I have to stop and start praying that no one but the Lord and I have control over me. There are people who can give me advice and show concern, guide me, but ultimately I have to make the decision about what to take from them.

Actually I had a long dream the other night about Robert Mack. He was going into great detail about how I could not write a book. He always told me no one would believe me. He demeaned me by saying I wasn't smart enough, but I know differently.

Surely my children realize how much I hated the control over my life that lasted our entire marriage. Mostly I detested not living my beliefs as a Christian. Not ever exercising my rights as an individual happened to me day in and day out.

journal entry

I hope the children will know how I hated Robert Mack's control over everything about me the whole time we were married. I detested the most not being able to live my life as the Christian person I knew I was. Not being allowed to say "no" to sex served as another control over me. I'd take away the pain he heaped upon the children if I could, and wishing for them I could get out of the marriage.

When my shoulders and other parts of my body ache now, I have to start asking the Lord to help me through the pain and be thankful I am alive and able to enjoy my children. Now I can enjoy the new adventures, relationships and all the milestones my children are making each day.

The gulf between Martha Lou and me was mended eventually. We had some ups and downs but our relationship was good before she passed away not long ago. She came to all the children's high school graduations except the last three due to illness.

This book does not describe a happy marriage or the relationship a married couple should share. The Lord did bless me with seven sons and one daughter. Four grandchildren extend our family so far. I look forward to watching the spiritual growth of each of my children. They share a special bond among themselves and their own families. Career successes continue to progress causing joy and pride in my heart.

The Sherry Moss family today

My Sustainable Scripture

Psalms 91

1. He who dwelleth in the secret place on the Most High shall abide under the shadow of the Almighty.

2. I will say of the Lord, He is my refuge and my fortress, my God; in him will I trust.

3. Surely he shall deliver three from the
snare of the fowler, and from the noisome
pestilence.

4. He shall cover thee with his feathers, and under his wings shalt thou trust; his truth shall be thy shield and buckler.

5. Thou shalt not be afraid for the terror by night, nor for the arrow that flieth by day,

6. Nor for the pestilence that walketh in darkness, nor for the destruction that wasteth at noonday.

7. A thousand shall fall at thy side, and ten thousand at thy right hand, but it shall not
come near thee.

8. Only with thine eyes shalt thou behold and see the reward of the wicked.

9. Because thou hast made the Lord, who is my refuge, even the Most High, thy habitation,

10. There shall no evil befall thee, neither shall any plague come near thy dwelling.

11. For he shall give his angels charge over thee, to keep thee in all thy ways.

12. They shall bear thee up in their hands, lest thou dash thy foot against a stone.

13. Thou shalt tread upon the lion and adder; the young lion and the serpent shalt thou trample under feet.

14. Because he hath set his love upon me, therefore will I deliver him; I will set him on high, because he hath known my name.

15. He shall call upon me, and I will answer him. I will be with him in trouble; I will deliver him, and honor him.

16. With long life will I satisfy him, and show him my salvation.

My personal love for Jesus Christ grows stronger every day as I claim His unconditional love for myself and my family. The amazing, unbreakable bond I enjoy with my children blesses me constantly and completely.

My Scripture of Hope Today

Proverbs 31:25
Strength and dignity are my clothing,
and she smiles at the future.

A true husband loves his wife and would never hurt her in any way.

Are you the victim of abuse or do you know someone who suffers from abuse?

CALL   1-800-799-7233

The National Domestic Violence Hot line. They will direct you toward a local shelter for battered women.

If you have access to a computer, visit www.leavingabuse.com for detailed information about leaving an abuser.

Other ideas for assistance:

* Talk to a trust minister.

* Make an appointment for your child with a doctor and ask him for help. A doctor can call the NDV Hot line for you.

* Call 911 for the police, but have a **plan to leave and a safe place to stay.**

* Request help from a trusted neighbor. He or she can call the NDV Hotline for you.

Notes:
(1) Bill Gothard Resigns Amid Sexual Harassment Investigation: Christianity Today, Feb. 2014
(2) Patriot Leader Bo Grits Shoots Himself Under Troubling Circumstances: Southern Poverty Law Center, Fall 1998.

Acknowledgements:
A special thank you to Kerri Lowrie, Janie Allen Wigley, Judy Allen, and Joe Taylor for spending hours creating my handwritten journal into a typed manuscript.

Judy Allen, editor
Joe Taylor, illustrator